FATHER'S
Love Letter

FATHER'S
Love Letter

Barry Adams

CHRISTIAN PUBLICATIONS, INC.

CAMP HILL, PENNSYLVANIA

✠ CHRISTIAN PUBLICATIONS, INC.

3825 Hartzdale Drive, Camp Hill, PA 17011
www.christianpublications.com

Faithful, biblical publishing since 1883

Father's Love Letter
ISBN: 0-87509-999-8
LOC Control Number: 2003105207
© 2003 by Barry Adams
All rights reserved
Printed in Korea

03   04   05   06   07   5   4   3   2   1

Author photo courtesy of
Bryan Macaulay of Village Studio.

Preface

The Story Behind "Father's Love Letter"

In October 1997 I responded to a call for pastors to come forward and receive prayer at a conference. The young man who prayed for me simply said, "I see a picture—you are a little baby and God is your Father, and right now He is reattaching your umbilical cord to Himself."

While I didn't see fireworks or feel anything dramatic, that was the beginning of my quest to know God more intimately as my heavenly Father. Over the next nine months I read every possible book and went to every meeting that dealt with the Father-heart of God.

In June 1998 I attended a men's retreat in North Bay, Ontario, where the weekend's goal was to get to know God more intimately as a Father. Near the end of the weekend, the speaker, Jack Winter, asked if I wanted prayer to receive a deeper revelation of the Father's love for me. As Jack prayed, I began to feel all the pain and disappointment of a little boy just wanting to be loved. In contrast to the emptiness that I felt, I also felt the incredible warmth of God the Father wrapping His arms around me. Wave upon wave of the love of God began to touch the deepest places in my heart that had been so wounded and discouraged as a child.

While I always had a theological understanding of God as my Father, that was the first time I had such a powerful encounter with God that it impacted my body, soul and spirit.

After encountering God in such a powerful way, I began to see the Father's love everywhere I looked in the Bible. It was like the "lights had been turned on" and I could see the theme of the Father-heart of God throughout the entire Bible.

I remember the day I asked God to help me better comprehend His love in light of the Scriptures I was now seeing throughout the entire Bible. In my heart I immediately heard a still small voice say: "If you put the Scriptures in the right order, they will form a love letter."

That was December 1998, and by January 1999 I had compiled a series of paraphrased Scriptures into a PowerPoint® presentation accompanied by Brian Doerksen's song, "Faithful Father," that I played as a sermon illustration in my home church.

I was amazed at how the congregation began to respond to this simple message of the Father's love for each of us. Many of the people seemed to be having an intimate, powerful encounter with their heavenly Father.

Everywhere I played this simple presentation, the results were the same. I began to see in a deeper way the incredible need that we all have to be loved in a way that only God the Father can love us. It was then that I started to wonder if God had a bigger plan to share this love letter around the world.

By November 1999, our Web site, www.FathersLoveLetter.com, was launched. Then, by September 2000, the demands of this new ministry were such that I had to ask the church that I pastored to release my wife and me into full-time ministry to share the message of Father's love.

In the past three years we have literally seen millions of visitors come to our Web site from over 125 nations to experience "Father's Love Letter" in over forty different languages. Our mandate today is the same as it was in January 1999: To simply deliver the love letter that God penned to a world that needs to hear and experience His incredible love.

Barry Adams
St. Catharines, Ontario

The words you are
about to read are true.

They will change your
life if you let them.

For they come from
the heart of God.

He loves you.

And He is the Father you
have been looking for all your life.

This is His love letter to you.

My Child . . .

You may not know me, but I know everything about you. I know when you sit down and when you rise up. I am familiar with all your ways. Even the very hairs on your head are numbered. For you were made in my image. In me you live and move and have your being. For you are my offspring. I knew you even before you were conceived. I chose you when I planned creation. You were not a mistake. For all your days are written in my book. I determined the exact time of your birth and where you would live. You are fearfully and wonderfully made. I knit you together in your mother's womb. And brought you forth on the day you were born. I have been misrepresented by those who don't know me. I am not distant and angry but am the complete expression of love. And it is my desire to lavish my love on you. Simply because you are my child and I am your Father. I offer you more than your earthly father ever could. For I am the perfect Father. Every good gift that you receive comes from my hand. For I am your provider and I meet all your needs. My plan for your future has always been filled with hope. Because I love you with an everlasting love. My thoughts toward you are countless as the sand on the seashore. And I rejoice over you with singing. I will never stop doing good to you. For you are my treasured possession. I desire to establish you with all my heart and all my soul. And I want to show you great and marvelous things. If you seek me with all your heart, you will find me. Delight in me and I will give you the desires of your heart. For it is I who gave you those desires. I am able to do more for you than you could possibly imagine. For I am your greatest encourager. I am also the Father who comforts you in all your troubles. When you are brokenhearted, I am close to you. As a shepherd carries a lamb, I have carried you close to my heart. One day I will wipe away every tear from your eyes. And I'll take away all the pain you have suffered on this earth. I am your Father, and I love you even as I love my son, Jesus. For in Jesus, my love for you is revealed. He is the exact representation of my being. He came to demonstrate that I am for you, not against you. And to tell you that I am not counting your sins. Jesus died so that you and I could be reconciled. His death was the ultimate expression of my love for you. I gave up everything I loved that I might gain your love. If you receive the gift of my son, Jesus, you receive me. And nothing will ever separate you from my love again. Come home and I'll throw the biggest party heaven has ever seen. I have always been Father and will always be Father. My question is . . . will you be my child? I am waiting for you.

Love, Your Dad
Almighty God

My child . . .

Matthew 18:1-4

God wants to pick you up, give you a hug and whisper your name in your ear. You are His child and He is your Father. This is your destiny; this is what you were created for. When you let Him love you in this way, as a father loves his little child, you will begin to realize that the need for love and affirmation you had as a little child is still deep within you. When you allow yourself to be embraced by God, you begin to see that this is what you've been looking for all your life. You may have searched for it in your career, in a relationship or in many other things, but you will find it only in one place—in the arms of your heavenly Father.

Prayer

Dear heavenly Father, I pray that You would give me the grace to become more childlike. I want You to pick me up and hold me tight. I want to lose myself in Your unfailing love. Help me to walk in the simplicity of faith that allows me to trust You wholeheartedly for *all* my needs. Thank You, gentle Father, for hearing this simple prayer. *Amen.*

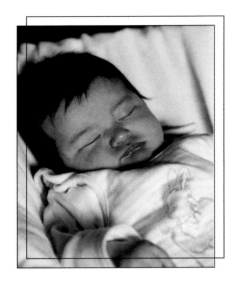

You may not know
me, but I know
everything
about you.

Psalm 139:1

Your Father knows you intimately. He knows your darkest fears and your brightest dreams. His love for you is higher and deeper and wider than any other love you have ever experienced in your entire life. The love that you are familiar with is usually conditional and based upon performance. But thanks be to God that His love is not an earthly love; it is divine in nature and not based upon your personal goodness but rather upon His goodness and mercy. Yes, your Father knows you, and He loves you with all His heart.

Prayer

Father, You know everything about me. You see all my bumps and bruises, yet You love me unconditionally. I thank You that Jesus paid the price for all my inadequacies so that I might come to You with complete confidence. I thank You that even though You know all about me and my shortcomings, You still love me as Your little child. Help me to walk in Your extravagant love today. *Amen.*

I know when you sit down and when you rise up.

Psalm 139:2

Your heavenly Father is intimately involved in every area of your life no matter how insignificant you might think it is. He is with you when you go to work; He is present when you play; and He watches over you when you sleep. No task that you set out to do in your daily routine is too mundane for your Father to take notice of. He has promised never to leave you or forsake you.

Though God is seated on His throne in heaven, He takes the time to watch over you because you are the object of His affection.

Prayer

Loving Father, You know everything about me. You watch over me twenty-four hours a day. You are everywhere all at once. I thank You that You are with me even in the most mundane aspects of my daily routine. I pray that as I go about my everyday activities, I will recognize Your abiding presence in all that I do. Thank You that You are never too busy to take time for me. *Amen.*

I am familiar with all your ways.

Psalm 139:3

Father God is fully acquainted with all that you are and all that you do. But the Father of all creation also wants you to see Him for who He really is. He wants you to know His Father-heart. To become intimate with someone requires vulnerability. That is why God made the first move to win your heart by sending His own dear Son to demonstrate His desire to be in a right relationship with you. When you receive the gift of God's Son into your life, you become an intimate partaker of the same divine relationship that Jesus enjoys with His Father.

Prayer

Father, I thank You for being familiar with all my ways. I believe that You understand *everything* about me, yet You still love me extravagantly. I want to know You, Father, more intimately than I have ever known You before. I want to begin to see into Your heart and to understand all *Your* ways. I pray this in the name of Your beloved Son, Jesus, who died on my behalf. *Amen.*

Even the *very hairs* on your head are numbered.

Matthew 10:29-31

The Father has taken the time to count each one of the hairs on your head. What incredible attention to detail! It is amazing to think that something so insignificant is important to God. The Father is so big that He can scoop the oceans in the palm of His hand, and yet His focus on you is so intense that He numbers each hair on your head. If there are days when you feel alone, when you think that no one really cares about you, remember that the Father has taken the time to count each hair on your head—not because He is bored or has nothing else to do but because you are His precious child.

Prayer

Father, I know You are in control of the world even when I feel that my life is out of control. Help me to trust in Your ability to care for each detail of my life. Thank You for loving me so much that You would take the time to count all the hairs on my head. I know You love me, and I believe that my worth to You is of great value. I pray that the reality of this truth will seep deeper into my heart today. *Amen.*

For you were made in my image.

Genesis 1:27

Even after God had created the heavens and the earth, something deep in His heart was not satisfied. So He proceeded to create man in His own image. The Bible says that God literally "breathed into [man's] nostrils the breath of life" (Genesis 2:7). What a tender moment it must have been when Adam took his first breath, opened his eyes and looked upon the loving gaze of his Father calling him to life. Just like Adam, there lies within you a divine DNA imprint that comes from God alone. You are one of God's children, and you have been created to reflect His image. What joy it must bring to the Father's heart when He sees His own likeness being mirrored in His precious creations.

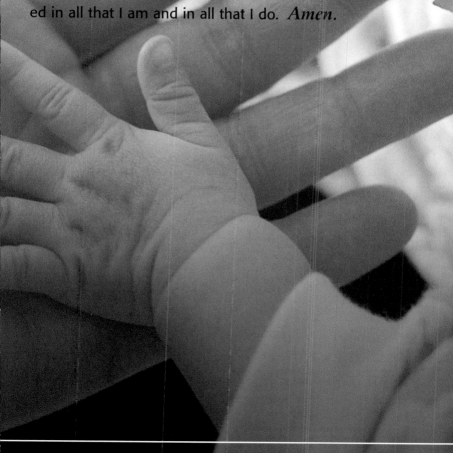

Prayer

Father, thank You for creating me in Your image. Help me to see the reflection of Your beauty in my life. Thank You for sustaining me by Your divine DNA imprint in my life. May Your likeness and the likeness of Your Son be reflected in all that I am and in all that I do. *Amen.*

In me you
live and move
and have
your being.

Acts 17:28

Though you were created by Father God to be a unique individual, you are really not a complete person until you claim your birthright as a child of God. Many people go through life unfulfilled because they have failed to receive the power and resources available to them through the Father. Don't squander the abundant and purposeful life God has promised to each of His children. He wants to shower you with blessing upon blessing. Yield to the Father's heart today.

Prayer

Father, I confess there are times when I'd rather go my own way—cut my own path through life. But so often I end up messing up my life. Help me to keep my eyes and heart focused on Your plan for my life. I don't want to miss out on Your many blessings. Thank You, Father, for Your love and forgiveness. *Amen.*

For you are my offspring.

Acts 17:28

Every person ever conceived came from God and was fashioned in His image. He is your Father; you are His offspring. He is the One who fathered you into life. This is true whether a person chooses to be identified as His child or not, for God's very essence is that of a loving Father. But God will never force His way into your life. You must make that conscious decision to accept Him as your Father. When you do, He will reach down, take your hand in His and never let it go. Father God loves you, His child, with an everlasting love.

Prayer

Heavenly Father, I gratefully acknowledge that You are my Father and I am Your child. How thankful I am that by choosing to receive Your love I will not pass into eternity without You. Help me feel Your pain for all the spiritually lost children who haven't yet found their way home to Your loving arms. Give me Your same compassion toward Your wayward offspring. *Amen.*

I knew you even before you were conceived.

Jeremiah 1:4-5

When Jeremiah was called to be a prophet to Israel, God told him that even before he had been conceived in his mother's womb, he was known by God and set apart for His divine purposes. Knowing this surely gave Jeremiah the strength to live out his destiny, even in the darkest of times. And the same is true for you. When everything else around you does not make sense, this bedrock truth can give you the assurance to keep going. What a wonderful thought—the God of the universe knows you intimately and set you apart for His purposes even before you were conceived!

*P*rayer

Father, it is truly humbling to know that Your amazing love for me existed even before I entered this world. You knew me and set me apart for Your special purpose long before I was born. Help me to receive a deeper revelation of this truth so that I might continue to live out my destiny in the shadow of Your love. *Amen.*

I chose you when I planned creation.

Ephesians 1:11-12

No one likes to be rejected. Perhaps you experienced rejection by your classmates or by your parents when you were a child. Even as adults, rejection can happen anytime and anywhere—in the workplace, at home or even in church. But God chose you to be His son or daughter from the very beginning of time. In the Father's eyes you are a precious treasure. He loves you and has a one-of-a-kind plan for your life.

*P*rayer

Father, thank You for choosing me to be part of Your forever family. I thank You that I am accepted unconditionally by the One who matters most. I desire to be Your child, to obey You in all things and to be a coheir with Jesus according to Your wonderful plan. Help me to fulfill the special purpose that was determined especially for me. *Amen.*

You were not a mistake.

Psalm 139:15-16

Through His Word, Father God has purposely communicated to you that your life is *not* a mistake. He lovingly watched as your yet-unformed body was woven together, and He took the time to carefully write down each one of your future days in His book. You are not just a population statistic in His eyes. You are a person who is incredibly unique, with a special purpose. You were not an accident, for you are loved more than you could ever know.

Prayer

Father, thank You that I have a special purpose in life and that all my days are written in Your book. Help me to always remember that You *wanted* me to come into this world and that You have planned each day that I live. Please grant to me a daily supply of strength and courage to sustain me. *Amen.*

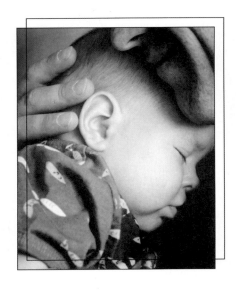

For all your days
are written
in my book.

Psalm 139:15-16

Most biographies are written *after* a person has fully lived his life and made some significant contribution to society. But, inconceivable as it may sound, God wrote your biography *before* you were born. What an all-knowing, all-powerful God! This same God who existed before time began and who knows all the events of the future is the loving Father who has personally invited you, His precious child, to live eternally with Him in His heavenly home.

Prayer

Almighty God, You already know more about me than I'll ever know about You. You have written out the perfect plan for my life. Enable me to be so in sync with Your Father-heart that my life will be a daily reflection of Your perfect will for me. *Amen.*

I determined the exact time of your birth and where you would live.

Acts 17:26

Did you know that you were born at the right time and at the right place? That's right. According to Scripture, God determined who your parents would be, the exact time you would be born and where you would live. He foresaw your life and placed you in your family. Father God will be with you through all the tough times, and His love will conquer even the most terrible of circumstances.

Prayer

Dear God, You chose my parents, the time of my birth and where I would live. I am thankful that You do not make mistakes. You are the perfect Master Planner. Help me to realize that Your love can penetrate any situation I face and that You desire to cause all things to work together for my good according to Your purposes. *Amen*.

You are fearfully and wonderfully made.

Psalm 139:14

Do you ever look in the mirror and wish you were different? Maybe you are too short or too tall, too thin or too heavy. The list never seems to end. Don't believe the lie that you have to look and act a certain way in order to be accepted. Your heavenly Father made you exactly the way He planned: your size, the color of your eyes—everything about you. The next time you look in the mirror, don't be afraid of what you see, for you were made in the image of God, and He declares that you are fearfully and wonderfully made.

Prayer

Father, forgive me for believing the lie that I have to be somebody other than who I am. The fact that You love and accept me is more important than love and acceptance from anyone else. I am thankful that I am Your child and that I am perfect in Your sight. *Amen.*

I knit you together in *your mother's* womb.

Psalm 139:13

It is amazing to consider how all-powerful God lovingly and tenderly created you. He could have simply blasted your shape out of rocks or snapped His fingers to create you. But instead He chose a more delicate process. Stitch by stitch and loop by loop, each one of your parts was carefully knit together by Almighty God. Your life is not the product of an impersonal evolution but the result of a loving Father who planned your creation before the foundations of the world. You are a masterpiece, and your very existence brings much joy to your Father's heart.

*P*rayer

Father, thank You for creating my inmost being. I know that each strand of my DNA was fashioned by You—stitch by stitch, loop by loop—with a love that called me to life. I was created in love and for love. And in my heart I want to express my love back to You for being such a wonderful Father. *Amen.*

And brought you forth on the day you were born.

Psalm 71:6

On the day you were born, God wasn't somewhere else tending to more important business. No, Father God was there to welcome you into His wonderful world and to affirm your destiny as His child. And since that day He has not left you but has numbered each one of your days in His special book. As you reflect on the day you were born, be comforted to know that your Father was there, and He was the proudest Papa of all!

Prayer

Heavenly Father, thank You for planning my creation since before the foundation of the world and for calling me to life. You have always been there for me, from the day of my birth, and You will always be there for me. Your love and acceptance is the bedrock of my life, and I will ever praise You! *Amen.*

I have been
misrepresented
by those who
don't know me.

John 8:41-44

Many people today struggle with misconceptions about God. Some see Him as an impersonal cosmic rule-giver; others picture Him as an emotionally distant earthly father. If you really want to know what Father is like, all you have to do is look at His Son, Jesus. All of Jesus' acts of compassion and kindness were pure expressions of His Father's true nature. So don't be fooled—God is the Father you've been looking for all your life!

Prayer

Father, I want to know You for who You really are. I want to see You as You are, not as I thought You to be. I repent of every lie that I have believed about You. You are a loving Father. Thank You for revealing Your true nature to me through the life of Your Son, Jesus. *Amen.*

I am not distant and angry but am the complete expression of love.

1 John 4:16

A few years ago there was a popular song that said that God was watching the world from a distance. The truth is that God is closer to you than you could possibly imagine. The Bible says, "God is love" (1 John 4:8). That concept is the foundation of the gospel. His love overflows to His children so that they can love Him back and have the ability to love others, too. He wants you to bask in His loving presence so that His love can touch the deepest need of your heart.

Prayer

Father, I acknowledge that You are the complete expres-sion of love. Thank You that Your love for me is uncondi-tional and without limit. I pray for an increased capacity for my heart to soak in Your sumptuous love every day, causing it to fill up, overflow and spill into every person that I meet. *Amen.*

And it is
my desire
to lavish
my love
on you.

1 John 3:1

What a thought: the God who created the heavens and the Earth has welcomed *you* into His glorious family! First and foremost you are His child, dearly loved of the Father. Your work or ministry involvements are secondary to this fact. He adores the real you! So before you get too busy in your daily routine, take a moment and meditate on the great love that the Father has lavished on you. What a privilege it is to be one of His cherished children!

Prayer

Heavenly Father, I thank You for the extravagant love that You pour out on me each day. Please remind me that I am Your child first, and then I am Your servant. I pray that You would remove any hindrances that would prevent me from receiving Your personal and intimate affection for me. I am so privileged to be called Your child. *Amen.*

Simply because you are my child and I am *your Father.*

1 John 3:1

It is incredible to think that you don't have to do anything auspicious to be a recipient of Father God's love and grace. You merely have to receive His offer of eternal life and put your trust in Him. What is even more incredible is the fact that not one person is deserving of this special gift that God offers. Yet, because the essence of the Father's heart is love, He freely offers this gift to all who will come. Such love deserves a response of adoration and obedience from a grateful child to his loving heavenly Father.

Prayer

Father, it seems so inadequate to merely use words to express my deepest thanks for Your incomparable gift of love and acceptance. I praise You for taking that huge first step toward reconciliation. You are the perfect example of what the relationship between Father and child should be. Thank You, Father, for Your unending goodness to me. *Amen.*

I offer you more than your earthly father ever could.

Matthew 7:9-11

God, who is the perfect parent, has placed within earthly fathers and mothers the natural desire to care for and to give good gifts to their children. Yet even the best meaning of parents, because they are beset with human flaws and imperfections, may at times disappoint their children. As loving as moms and dads can be, their hearts are marred by sin and tainted by selfish motives. Contrast this to the love of Father God: His is a limitless, holy, unconditional love! Your heavenly Father smiles every time He looks upon your face. It is almost humanly impossible to comprehend the incredible love that Father God has for you.

Prayer

Father, I confess that I have related to You in the same way that I have related to my earthly father. Help me to see the truth that You love me *much more* than my earthly father ever could. I come to You today with my needs because I know that You love me unconditionally and want to give me good gifts! *Amen.*

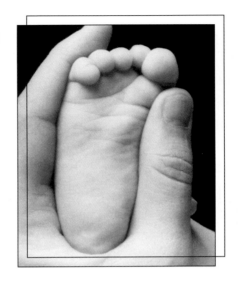

For I am *the perfect* Father.

Matthew 5:48

God's children are created to be loved perfectly. That may be a difficult concept to grasp in today's world, but it is nonetheless true that woven into the fabric of a child's inner being is an expectation to be loved unconditionally. As children grow up they begin to see their parents' humanity, which sometimes leads to a sense of disillusionment. Yet God is not like our earthly parents. The Bible says that He is the Perfect Father. He will not let you down. He will not dissatisfy you. He is perfect in every way. God is the Father that you have always needed.

Prayer

Perfect Father, today I choose to forgive my earthly parents for not meeting all my love needs. I love them despite their human faults and blemishes. Thank You that You love me perfectly in spite of my own failings. And help me to love more perfectly, like You, in all of my relationships. *Amen.*

Every good gift that you receive comes from my hand.

James 1:17

Every good and perfect gift that you receive comes from the hand of God. Your life, your family, your talents. Father God is the giver of good gifts and He never changes. He is the same yesterday, today and forever. His love is not fickle or conditional. He loves to give good gifts to the ones He adores. He is the most generous Person in the universe. Your life is a precious gift from your heavenly Father who loves you and will never fail you. He is completely faithful and dependable.

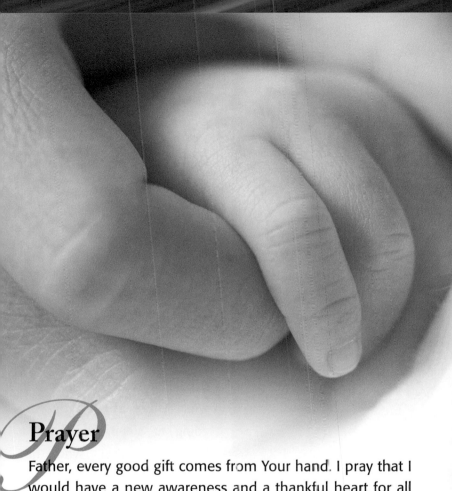

Prayer

Father, every good gift comes from Your hand. I pray that I would have a new awareness and a thankful heart for all that You freely give to me. May each sunset remind me of the beautiful canvas You have painted for my enjoyment. I am thankful that You do not change and that Your love is something I can rely on every day of my life. *Amen.*

For I am your provider and I meet all your needs.

Matthew 6:31-33

One of the biggest causes of stress in life is the pressure to provide for daily needs. Parents are especially strapped with these practical concerns. But Father God wants you to rely on Him so that He will be the main provider in your life. You don't have to worry and strive about what you are going to eat, what you are going to wear and where you are going to sleep. You have a heavenly Father who has promised to look after all the nitty-gritty details of your life.

Prayer

Father, I confess that I have been anxious about many things. Help me to trust You with today's provision and to leave tomorrow's needs in Your care. I want to seek *You* first today. I have confidence and faith that You will provide for all of my needs—and more! *Amen.*

My plan for your future has always been filled with hope.

Jeremiah 29:11

Wars, famine, pollution, recessions, etc., can cause people to become easily discouraged when they look at the future. The world can seem like a place devoid of hope. But the good news is that your hope is not based on circumstances but in God the Father. That does not necessarily mean that life will always turn out the way you expect or want, but it does mean that you can always trust in Father God to love you and watch over you. If you commit your life into His care, you are guaranteed, from an everlasting perspective, that you will have an incredible future filled with hope awaiting you. And it is going to last forever!

Prayer

Father, thank You that whatever my earthly circumstances, I need not fear nor despair, for You are in ultimate control of my life. Help me to commit my life to You, trusting in Your faithfulness to accomplish all that You have promised to do. I thank You that Your plan for me is filled with hope and a future. *Amen.*

Because I love you with an everlasting love.

Jeremiah 31:3

Everything that Father God does is motivated by His everlasting love for you. His love is perpetual, unending, eternal. There was never a time in all of eternity when you were not loved by God. Nothing you can do can make God love you any more—or any less—than He does right now. You may have an intellectual understanding that God loves you, but He desires for this revelation to seep into every fabric of your being—especially into your heart.

Prayer

Father, I praise You for loving me with a love that will never run out or dry up. I want to experience Your love in a deeper way than I have ever experienced it before. I pray that my heart may be rooted and established in Your love and that I might have power to grasp how wide and how long and how high and how deep is Your love for me expressed in the person of Your Son, Jesus Christ. *Amen.*

My thoughts
toward you are
countless as the sand
on the seashore.

Psalm 139:17-18

Have you ever tried to count the individual grains of sand on the seashore? It is incomprehensible to think that anyone could ever count them all. But the Bible says that God's thoughts about you actually outnumber the grains of sand on the seashore. Practically speaking, this means that your heavenly Father *never* stops thinking about you. Moreover, His thoughts are not of condemnation and judgment but thoughts of absolute love and adoration. What a faithful and ever-loving Father!

Prayer

Ever-loving Father, it amazes me that Your thoughts toward me outnumber the grains of sand on the seashore. It is mind-boggling to know that the Creator of the universe never stops thinking about me! I pray that I might be able to receive this truth into my heart so that I can respond with loving thoughts back to You. *Amen*.

And I rejoice over you with singing.

Zephaniah 3:17

Your heavenly Father takes great delight in your life. The Bible says that He rejoices over you with singing. His song of love proclaims to the heavens His undying affection toward you. He is not ashamed of His love for you, and He wants the whole universe to know it. The next time you worship the Father in song, remember that as you sing of your love for Him, He in turn sings His song of love for you.

Prayer

Father, I pray that You will give me ears to hear Your love songs for me. I pray that I will be able to silence the busy-ness of my life so I can hear Your soothing lullabies and Your bellowing melodies. Thank You for being with me and for taking such great delight in my life. *Amen.*

I will never stop doing good to you.

Jeremiah 32:40

Father God has made an ever-lasting covenant with you. His covenant is irrevocable and everlasting.

He promises to never stop doing good to you. Never. His promise is true because He is faithful to keep His word. God's word is His bond. Whenever you feel that everybody and everything is against you, be reminded that your Father in heaven is always on your side.

Prayer

Father, I thank You that You will never stop doing good to me. Your word is Your bond, and I choose to believe Your word to be true. Even when I don't feel like it, I pray that You will open my eyes to see all the goodness that surrounds me. *Amen.*

For you are *my treasured* possession.

Exodus 19:5

You must be incredibly valuable to God, for He paid the highest price that could be paid for your redemption—the life of His only Son. The God who made all the precious jewels, the gold and the silver, has chosen you to be His most treasured possession. Your worth is not based on what you think of yourself or on your own good deeds, but solely on the astronomical price that God was willing to pay for you to come home. You are of greater worth to the Father than the most stunning treasures imaginable. May you never forget the value of the gift the Father gave you when He sacrificed His beloved Son, Jesus, on your behalf.

Prayer

Father, I receive the love gift of Your Son, Jesus, as the price You paid in order to purchase my redemption. I acknowledge that my worth does not come from what I do, but simply because of whose I am. Because of Jesus, I am accepted as Your child and am Your most treasured possession. I praise You and thank You. *Amen.*

I desire to establish you with all my heart and all my soul.

Jeremiah 32:41

When Father God declared that He loved you, He didn't do it halfheartedly. He planted you in His love with *all* His heart and soul. The love that God demonstrates does not go halfway but is fully committed to giving you everything and not holding back anything. He has fully committed His heart and His soul to you, and the only thing that He asks of you in return is that you will respond by simply loving Him back. Father God has already proved His love to you, giving up all that He loved. But the question for you to ponder remains: Will you respond to His initiation of love and love Him in return with *all* your heart and *all* your soul? He is waiting.

Prayer

Father, I thank You that You rejoice in doing good for me and have committed *all* that You have to me. In response to the initiation of Your love for me, I give You all that I have and all that I am in return. You are a wonderful Father and I am so privileged to be Your child. *Amen.*

And I want
to show you
great and
marvelous things.

Jeremiah 33:3

Your Father in heaven desires to reveal His heart to you. Any time, night or day, you can go to Him with your questions and concerns with complete confidence, knowing that He promises to answer you and tell you great and unsearchable things. When you call out to your Father God, He is always faithful to answer your cry and to reveal the mysteries of His kingdom. He will never turn you away. Nor will He forbid you from asking too many questions. He delights to have you in His presence at all times.

Prayer

Heavenly Father, You are to be praised for Your great patience with me! Whenever I call out to You, You give me Your undivided attention. I come to You now with an expectant heart, ready to sit down on Your lap so that You might unlock the mysteries of this journey called life. Thank You that You are never too tired to listen to my many questions. I love You. *Amen.*

If you seek me with all your heart, you will find me.

Deuteronomy 4:29

The Bible says that if you pursue the Lord with everything you have, He promises you will find Him. When you search for Him, He never hides Himself so that He cannot be found. Plain and simple, Father God *wants* to be found by you. What an outrageous statement! This means that you don't need to have a seminary degree, live a sinless life or say some magic words to gain access to the Creator of the world. If you truly desire to know God more intimately, He will make Himself known to you.

Prayer

Father, I am thankful that You do not make it difficult for me to find You, for You are never far away and are always overjoyed to be found. I pray that I might pursue You with all my heart and soul, all the while having a childlike anticipation of finding You. I desire to know You more intimately. *Amen.*

Delight in me and I will give you the desires of your heart.

Psalm 37:4

Father God loves you and wants to give you the desires of your heart. Scripture says that if you simply delight in God and enjoy His friendship, He will give you the desires of your heart. The desires that God is referring to are not your momentary impulses but the deep-seated longings in your heart that are in accordance with His will. Nothing pleases your heavenly Father more than to grant His children the desires of their hearts. So take pleasure in the Father's love today—and watch what happens!

Prayer

Father, I want to take the time to delight in You today. You are a wonderful Father and I love You with all my heart! Thank You for making me the way I am and for promising to give me the secret desires of my heart. I trust in Your divine timing, and I commit all my dreams and plans into Your tender care. *Amen.*

For it is I who gave you *those desires.*

Philippians 2:13

God is the Master Architect of your life. He equips you with all you need to accomplish what He has foreordained for your life. He's a Father who loves diversity and who uses your distinctive desires to guide you to do His will. He is the One who designed your DNA and who works in you to will and to act according to His good purposes. Isn't it wonderful to know that there is a Master Designer who has crafted you uniquely to carry out His special plan for your life?

Prayer

Father God, thank You for placing godly desires in my heart. I know that You work in me to will and to act according to Your good purposes. Please open my inner eyes to see when my desires and Your desires are in perfect unison in my life. *Amen.*

I am able to do more for you than you could possibly imagine.

Ephesians 3:20-21

Try to think of something way beyond your wildest dreams. Even if you have a vivid imagination, there will still be a limit to what you are able to comprehend. However, Father God does not have the same limitations that you have. He knows no earthly barriers or boundaries that will keep Him from fulfilling the best plans and purposes for His children. God is able to do immeasurably more than all you ask or imagine according to His power that is at work within you!

Prayer

Father, You are the biggest, strongest and most wonderful Dad in the universe! I know that You love me and have a plan for me that is immeasurably more than I could possibly imagine. Thank You for giving me Your precious Holy Spirit who is at work in me to fulfill all that You have purposed for me. Help me to believe in You for greater things in my life than my own human limitations can comprehend. *Amen.*

For I am your greatest *encourager.*

2 Thessalonians 2:16-17

Father God is your greatest encourager! He has not come to condemn you but to encourage you. He speaks hope into the deepest part of your being. He stands on the sidelines cheering you on as you race down the field of life. His shouts of encouragement provide you with all the strength you will need in order to finish the race that was uniquely charted for you.

Prayer

Father, thank You for Your loving glance and encouraging words. I know that You want to see me finish well. Thank You for running the race of life alongside of me and for picking me up whenever I fall down. I am especially thankful that through Your Son, Jesus, I have been empowered to run the race that You have laid out for me. *Amen.*

I am also the Father who comforts you in all your troubles.

2 Corinthians 1:3-4

God is the Father of compassion and of all comfort. When you need comfort most, He is faithful to be by your side through all your pain and disappointment. He weeps with you, and His heart breaks with yours. Your heavenly Father wants to hold your hand as you walk through the seasons in your life. You were never meant to shoulder these burdens on your own. Father God wants to comfort you with His tender love so that you can pass on the comfort you have received to others when they are in need.

Prayer

Father, thank You for always being there for me in all my troubles. You are the Father of compassion and the God of all comfort. When I am in despair, I know You are close to me. Help me to feel Your arms of love around me, sustaining and comforting me in my deepest time of need. *Amen.*

When you are broken-hearted, I am close to you.

Psalm 34:18

At your greatest time of need, when you feel the most alone, Father God is very close to you. When your heart is broken in pieces, He is very near, bringing comfort and healing. You may not always feel His presence during difficult times, but He is with you nonetheless. Father's heart is deeply moved with compassion for you, and He wants to revive you when you are crushed in your spirit.

Prayer

Father, when I am bruised and broken, I am encouraged to know that You are near. I pray that I might allow Your arms of love to surround me in the midst of my brokenness and despair. I know that during the most difficult seasons in my life, You are close to me. Thank You for drawing near to me and for saving me in my greatest time of need. *Amen.*

As a shepherd carries a lamb, I have *carried you close* to my heart.

Isaiah 40:11

The Bible uses the word picture of a loving shepherd caring for his flock of sheep to illustrate God's desire for intimacy with mankind. Imagine the look on the shepherd's face as he lovingly gazes down into the eyes of each lamb he holds close to his breast. There is no other place that these lambs would rather be at that moment in time. What a picture of intimacy and safety! Their shepherd cares for them and has vowed to lay his life down for their protection. That is exactly how God wants to relate to you. He is your Shepherd, and you are His little lamb whom He dearly loves and wants to protect.

Prayer

Loving Father, pick me up and hold me in Your strong arms. I want to hear the beating of Your heart and feel the warmth and safety of Your embrace. You are the Great Shepherd, and I am just a little lamb who needs to be held. Thank You for holding me close to Your heart. *Amen.*

One day I will wipe away every tear from your eyes.

Revelation 21:3-4

The Bible promises to those who put their faith in Christ that at the end of all time there will be no more death or mourning, no more crying or pain. The soothing comfort of Father God's love will assuredly make all your earthly suffering a distant memory. And as He gazes into your tear-filled eyes, you will realize at that moment that you are finally home. While your temporal life on earth will one day come to an end, you have the hope of an eternity of living near to the Father's heart.

Prayer

Father, it is hard for gravity-bound earthlings to imagine what heaven will be like—no more death or pain or injustices or hatred. I look forward to that day when I will see You face-to-face and dwell with You forever. Thank You for the incredible hope that I have because of the willingness of Jesus to bear my sins on the cross. *Amen.*

And I'll
take away
all the pain you have suffered on this earth.

Revelation 21:3-4

If there is one common denominator to be found in the world over the course of history, it is the presence of physical and emotional pain in people's lives. Suffering is a normal part of human existence. It touches nearly every family. But your heavenly Father has prepared a place for His children where pain and suffering will be extinct. Instead of pain there will be the fullness of love and goodness. As one of His favored children, you will luxuriate in the sunshine of His Father-love, and you will never again know the shadow of suffering and loss. Its memory will be lost in the halls of eternity.

Prayer

Heavenly Father, I so much look forward to that day when there will be no more pain and suffering, when I will be surrounded by Your loving presence. But so many of my loved ones do not know about this place that You have prepared. Help me, Lord, to be a better communicator of Your love and grace to those who are experiencing pain and who have no hope for a better future. *Amen.*

I am your Father, and I love you even as I love my son, Jesus.

John 17:23

Jesus is the ideal Son that any Father would be proud of. He was sinless and perfect in every way and obedient to His Father's every wish. Theirs is the ultimate love relationship—the perfect Son and the perfect Father. What is incredible to consider is that because of the cross, you have the privilege of sharing in the same relationship with the Father that Jesus has had from the beginning of time. When the Father looks at you, He sees the life of His beloved Son! You may not be able to comprehend this incredible love, and it is not something that you could ever earn, but it is yours by faith through Jesus Christ. God loves you even as He loves Jesus!

Prayer

Loving Father, I pray that You will help me grasp the amazing truth that You love me even as You love Your Son, Jesus. Though it is difficult to comprehend, by faith I believe it to be true. I praise You that You have welcomed me with open arms into Your forever family. *Amen.*

For in Jesus, my love for you is revealed.

John 17:26

Jesus desired that you would know and experience His Father's heart just as He had known and experienced this amazing love from the very beginning. How awesome to think that Jesus was willing to leave the intimacy and glory of His Father's presence to make the Father known to you! Through the cross, Jesus has made the way for *you* to be a joint heir with Him as a son or a daughter to His Father. What a privilege to be a partaker of the Father's incredible love!

*P*rayer

Father, thank You for sending Your only Son, Jesus, to reveal Your amazing love for me. I am overwhelmed at the truth that I can share in the same relationship with You that Jesus has had with You from the very beginning. By faith I receive Your love through the life of my Savior and Lord, Jesus Christ. *Amen.*

He is the *exact representation* of my being.

Hebrews 1:3

When Jesus walked this earth, many people had a distorted image of the true nature of God. It is no different today than it was 2,000 years ago. Many still suffer from false beliefs about God's character. Jesus came to dispel those false beliefs and to truly reveal His Father's heart. If you want to know what your heavenly Father is really like, just look into the eyes of Jesus and let His love melt away all your misconceptions.

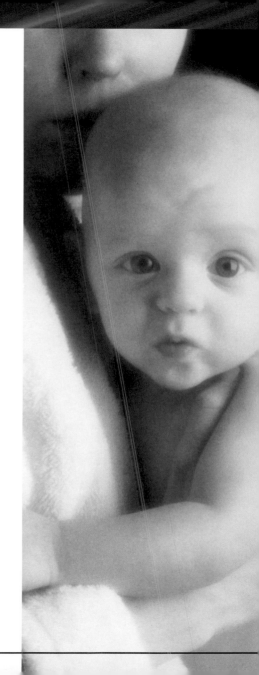

*P*rayer

Father, thank You for sending Your only Son, Jesus, to show me what You are really like. I believe that He is the exact representation of Your being and the radiance of Your glory. Help me to see Your Father's heart in every compassionate act of love and mercy that Jesus demonstrated. *Amen.*

He came to demonstrate that I am for you, not against you.

Romans 8:31

At times in your life you have probably encountered people and obstacles that seem to be going in a different direction than you. This can be a very discouraging and lonely reality. The truth is that God is for you, not against you. Not only is He on your side, but He is cheering you on as He plans great things for your life. You can be confident that your heavenly Daddy is the biggest, strongest, most loving Person in the universe and has declared to the heavens that He is for you!

Prayer

Father, I admit that sometimes I feel as though the whole world is against me. But I thank You that Your love causes all things to work together for my good. Jesus demonstrated Your love for me and has convinced me of Your unfailing acceptance and affection. I thank You that I will forever be Your child. *Amen.*

And to tell you that I am not *counting* your sins.

2 Corinthians 5:18-19

Father God is righteous and holy and therefore sin cannot dwell in His presence. This presents a problem for humans, who are born with a sin nature. Therefore, by God's great mercy, mankind's sinfulness was dealt with once and for all by the death of Jesus Christ. Because of the cross, when God looks at His children, He does not see their sin but only the precious blood of His Son, Jesus. Because of Jesus' sacrifice, you have been reconciled to God. What a glorious thought: God does not count your sins against you!

Prayer

Father, I believe that You are not an angry judge, but You are my loving Father. I thank You for sending Your Son, Jesus Christ, to die on a cross for me to take upon Himself all my sins. I thank You that His death, burial and resurrection have made a way for me to be completely forgiven and fully reconciled to You as Your little child. *Amen.*

Jesus died so that you and I could be reconciled.

2 Corinthians 5:18-19

Almighty God sent His Son, Jesus, into the world so that you could be fully reconciled to the Father's heart. If you have believed in Jesus Christ and accepted His gift of salvation, you can be assured that you are fully reconciled to Father God. You are not His slave or a serf but one of His sons. The curtain that once separated you from a Holy God has been torn in two. You are one of His prized, redeemed children!

Prayer

Father, thank You that Jesus made a way for me to be fully reconciled with You. As a wayward child makes the journey home, today I return into Your loving arms of acceptance and restoration. This is where I belong, and this is where I was destined to dwell all the days of my life. *Amen.*

His death was the ultimate expression of my love for you.

1 John 4:10

It is one thing to say the words "I love you," but it is quite another thing to *prove* your love. God not only said that He loved us; He demonstrated it practically by sending us His only Son as an atoning sacrifice for our sins. When you struggle to believe that God loves you, you need not go any farther than the cross to see the full expression of His love. You are absolutely and completely loved by God. May the cross of Christ serve as an eternal token of the Father's affection for you.

Prayer

Father, please forgive me for the times when I have questioned Your love for me. I believe that You have demonstrated that love once and for all through the cross of Christ. I pray that the truth of Your love for me will be the bedrock of my faith even during the times that I don't feel loved. *Amen.*

I gave up everything I loved that I might *gain your love.*

Romans 8:32

The apple of the Father's eye was His one and only Son, Jesus. Nothing could ever separate them from the love they had for each other. Yet there came a time when they were physically separated, when Jesus left the safety of heaven and His Father's right side to take on the form of a helpless little baby. But throughout that time, they still remained one in heart and in Spirit. Then the unthinkable happened: The Son of God, who knew no sin, voluntarily took upon Himself the cumulative sin of the entire world. In the darkest moment in all of history, Jesus bore the weight of humanity's ugliness upon a crude cross. Father God gave up all that He loved in order to gain our love. If He did not spare His dearest Treasure in order to win our freedom, how much more is He willing to graciously give us all things?

Prayer

Merciful Father, thank You for not sparing Your only Son so that I could receive an eternal inheritance. You gave up everything that You loved in order to gain my love. You have proven Your unfailing love to me. Forgive me for ever doubting that You love me. I willingly give my whole heart to You. *Amen.*

If you receive the gift of my son, Jesus, you receive me.

1 John 2:23

The Father and the Son are one. All that belongs to the Father is the Son's, and all that belongs to the Son is the Father's. This means that you have complete and unrestricted access to the Father. You need not ever feel that you are missing anything if you have asked Jesus to come into your life. When you receive the Son, you receive His Father. If Jesus lives in you, then the Father lives in you, and He has given His Holy Spirit as a deposit guaranteeing your inheritance. What a joy it is to be in a relationship with all three Persons of the Trinity!

Prayer

Father, thank You that when I received the gift of Your Son, Jesus, I received all that You have to offer. Thank You for coming to live in me when I asked Jesus into my heart. I love You and want to know You more deeply than I have ever known You before. *Amen.*

And nothing will ever
separate you
from my
love again.

Romans 8:38-39

The Bible says that nothing in all creation can separate you from the love of God. It is especially in times of intense grieving and loss that you may need to be reminded of this glorious truth. Your loving Father has made a way through the gift of His Son for you to experience His closeness in every situation and for all eternity. No power in heaven or on the earth can separate you from His love—not even death. Because through Jesus Christ there is the promise of eternal life for His children. If you are His child today, your tomorrows are filled with Father's perpetual presence and love.

Prayer

Father, Your love for me is more powerful than anything in creation—past, present or future. I pray that all of the barriers that I have put up in my life that have separated me from Your love would be removed right now so that I might experience the fullness of Your love—for all eternity. *Amen.*

Come home
and I'll throw
the biggest party
heaven has ever seen.

Luke 15:7

In the story of the prodigal son recorded in Luke 15, the returning son expected harsh judgment but received a party instead! Time and time again the Father surprises us with His offer to celebrate over a lost one's return to His house. Father God loves throwing parties for His kids, for each party represents an orphan or prodigal who has found his way back into His heart. The heart of the Father is rich in mercy and grace, and He is wooing His wayward children to come home to join in the party!

Prayer

Father, how marvelous it is that You love to celebrate when a lost child comes home. I was once a lost child, but You cared enough to throw me a party upon my return home. Help me to feel Your heart for each prodigal who returns home so that I can join in their party. *Amen.*

I have always been Father and will always be Father.

Ephesians 3:14-15

God is not only the Author of all creation but is Father over His family in heaven and on earth. While the name "Creator" describes what He does, the name "Father" describes who He is. And He doesn't want to be known just as an impersonal Father over all creation but wants to be known as your own personal Daddy. As the revelation of God's Fatherhood becomes more and more real in your own heart, you will be more apt to cry out to Father God in the same way as a little child calls out to his earthly father: "Papa!" "Daddy!" He is waiting to hear the cry of your voice.

Prayer

Father, I thank You that You are my Daddy, my heavenly Father, my God. You have not given me a spirit that makes me a slave to fear, but You have given me a spirit of adoption so that I am able to cry, "Father!" I pray that Your Holy Spirit would continue to witness with my spirit that I am Your little child. *Amen.*

My question is . . . will you be *my child?*

John 1:12-13

Have you received the gift of God's only Son, or have you put off that decision? It is your choice to make. Father God is not willing that even one person should reject this precious gift, but He will never overpower your freedom of choice. This gift is freely given and it must be freely received. Being born of God is the most wonderful experience that can ever happen to a human being. It is the ultimate homecoming that you have been created for: to be welcomed as a son or a daughter in Father God's glorious family.

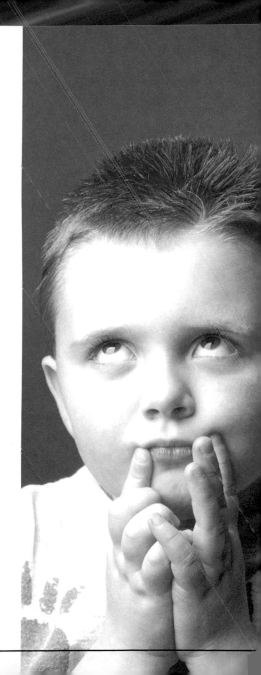

*P*rayer

Father, I want to be Your child. I believe that Jesus Christ died for me, and I gladly receive Him as my Savior and Lord. Thank You, Jesus, for being obedient to Your Father's will by dying on the cross for me. Thank You for taking upon Yourself *my* sin and *my* shame. I turn from my own way of doing things. Come into my heart, Lord Jesus. Today I am coming home! *Amen.*

I am waiting for you.

Luke 15:11-24*

Father God is waiting anxiously for the return of every lost child who is wandering aimlessly without hope and without Father's love. If you have strayed away from the Father's love, He is waiting for you with outstretched arms. He will not force you to come home, because that would violate your freedom of choice. Father God is waiting for you to come home so He can throw you a party. So don't waste any more time. Come home to the love you have been looking for all your life. Your Father's arms are aching to hold you.

*See appendix for complete biblical text.

Prayer

Loving Father, even though I have sinned and turned away from Your love, You have been patiently waiting for me to come home. Your love has won my heart, so I return into Your loving arms. This is where I have always belonged and where I will stay for the rest of my life. It feels so good to finally be home. *Amen*.

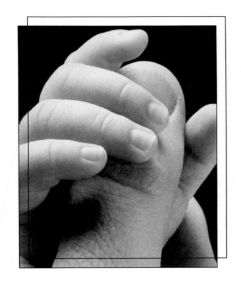

<hr />

Love,
Your Dad
Almighty God

<hr />

This signature expresses both the majesty of a holy God and the tenderness of a loving Father. There is a tendency to gravitate toward one concept of God or the other. But the truth is that both concepts are correct. For you are infinitely loved by One who is righteous and omnipotent yet who also is tender and abounding in love. The Almighty God is also your Heavenly Dad! The One who created the heavens and the earth took the time to knit you together in your mother's womb. The One who makes nations tremble and who holds the hearts of kings in His hands wants you to come close to Him to hear the beating of His heart. What an awesome heavenly Father!

Prayer

Dear Father, You are Almighty God, and yet You are the loving Father I have been looking for all my life. I receive Your gift of love expressed through the death, burial and resurrection of Jesus Christ. Thank You for making me a coheir with Your Son, Jesus, in Your glorious inheritance. I will be ever grateful that I am loved and accepted as Your child. *Amen.*

Appendix

The Parable of the Lost Son

Luke 15:11-24

Jesus continued: "There was a man who had two sons. The younger one said to his father, 'Father, give me my share of the estate.' So he divided his property between them.

"Not long after that, the younger son got together all he had, set off for a distant country and there squandered his wealth in wild living. After he had spent everything, there was a severe famine in that whole country, and he began to be in need. So he went and hired himself out to a citizen of that country, who sent him to his fields to feed pigs. He longed to fill his stomach with the pods that the pigs were eating, but no one gave him anything.

"When he came to his senses, he said, 'How many of my father's hired men have food to spare, and here I am starving to death! I will set out and go back to my father and say to him: Father, I have sinned against heaven and against you. I am no longer worthy to be called your son; make me like one of your hired men.' So he got up and went to his father.

"But while he was still a long way off, his father saw him and was filled with compassion for him; he ran to his son, threw his arms around him and kissed him.

"The son said to him, 'Father, I have sinned against heaven and against you. I am no longer worthy to be called your son.'

"But the father said to his servants, 'Quick! Bring the best robe and put it on him. Put a ring on his finger and sandals on his feet. Bring the fattened calf and kill it. Let's have a feast and celebrate. For this son of mine was dead and is alive again; he was lost and is found.' So they began to celebrate.

Barry Adams was an associate pastor at Westview Christian Fellowship when he first presented "Father's Love Letter" as a sermon illustration in January 1999. He is the cofounder of Father Heart Communications with his wife Anneliese, and they both serve as North American advisory board members for the Father's Love Forum. They live in St. Catharines, Ontario, with their three children, Kristin, Stephen and Candice.

To find out more about the ministry of "Father's Love Letter," visit:

www.𝕏FathersLoveLetter.com